How to be a
Good Parent

Compiled by Jaqueline Mitchell

Bodleian Library
UNIVERSITY OF OXFORD

This edition first published in 2015 by the Bodleian Library
Broad Street
Oxford OX1 3BG
www.bodleianshop.co.uk

ISBN: 978 1 85124 438 6

This edition © Bodleian Library, University of Oxford, 2015

Text abridged from sources on pp. 85–6

Images © Bodleian Library, University of Oxford, 2015

Images adapted from illustrations in catalogues from 1930–1939
taken from the John Johnson Collection in the Bodleian Library,
University of Oxford: Sewing Cottons and Sewing Machines 4 (9);
Women's Clothes and Millinery 10 (37); Women's Clothes and
Millinery 10 (5).

Cover design by Dot Little at the Bodleian Library
Designed and typeset by JCS Publishing Services Ltd in 9.5pt on
11.7pt Georgia font
Printed and bound in Italy by L.E.G.O. SpA

British Library Catalogue in Publishing Data
A CIP record of this publication is available from the British Library

NOTE TO READERS

THIS book is a compilation of instructions for
parents extracted from books written largely
in the first half of the twentieth century. At
this time, of course, it was generally assumed
that 'mother' would take the chief role in
raising the children. In order to preserve the
tone of these instruction books, we have on
the whole not attempted to replace 'mother'
with 'father' or 'parent', and it should be taken
as read that the advice offered is as likely to
be as useful to the father as the mother in the
twenty-first century. We have, however, in a
few instances taken the liberty of changing the
child's gender, where this is not specific to the
advice, and have lightly edited the extracts so
that the chapters read more smoothly.

CONTENTS

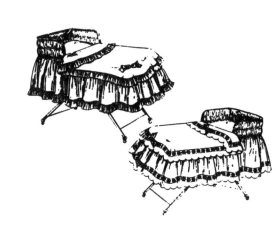

I

WHERE DO I BEGIN?

BEING A PARENT

THERE is no more responsible job than motherhood. There are more failures and more bunglers in this business of being a parent than in any other one phase of human activity. This is not a reflection on the parents; it is an admission that 'mothering' is, of all the difficult leader-roles, the most difficult.

The love of a mother for her child should be as near the perfect love as human nature can ever hope to be. But the love that so concerns itself with every thought, whim and need of the child can create a sense of dependence that engenders selfishness, vanity and laziness.

A mother's love should take account, at all times, of the needs of her child; but she must remember that whims are not needs!

A child who is picked up and petted after receiving a fall, or a child who is watched so closely that he never gets a fall, and the child who is entertained every moment of time, will never develop any *power of resistance or resourcefulness*. A resourceful child makes a resourceful grown-up and the most resourceful people are the happiest, for they find much to be happy in.

Don't, if you have a talented, a beautiful or an exceptional child, commit the heinous offence of 'spoiling' him! Conversely, it is unfair and unintelligent to discourage latent talent, or to belittle physical beauty, or to blind the eyes to precociousness.

It is safe to say that over-meddlesome people about a child will do much more harm than those who do too little. Everything with which the child comes in contact has an influence of some kind. It therefore behoves us all to have some elementary ideas of the ways in which we affect character in our relations with those under our care, and how immensely this will, later on, determine the relations of those persons with the world and themselves.

There is very little danger of internal family jealousies, which can disintegrate the whole scheme of happy family life, if the parents both realize their responsibilities towards the children they have chosen to create.

Parents should agree if possible on the methods of rearing their children, but if it is not possible to agree, then differences should be settled beyond the hearing of the child. Nothing will weaken the authority of both parents so much as for the child to know that they do not agree.

A child should not be ruled by fear of his parents but by love, though when loving measures fail to control, he should know that sterner measures will be adopted. There comes a time with all children when persuasive arguments will not avail and if they are humoured at this time the seed is sown for disobedience.

Tell your child that you love him. Do not make the mistake of leaving demonstrated affection out of your home life. This affection if realized will have a strong influence on your child all his life.

Remember in rearing your children that you reap what you sow.

THE FIVE GUIDING PRINCIPLES

Your object in the training and education of a child should be to form good habits about the *small things of daily life*: to teach him to be clean and nice in his personal ways, bright, and natural in manner, to eat his food prettily, to be industrious and neat, swift and cheerful to obey, truthful and open.

Love, patience, firmness, encouragement, explanation: these are the five great moral tools, or guiding principles, which we must thoroughly master and use.

Love is the first essential and the last because it should be never failing.

Patience. We must not expect to build brains, characters and souls as children build houses of bricks. Growth must be gradual, and patience is our great friend, we being content if each day shows even some slight improvement in a child. There will be many disappointments and back-slidings, which we must take calmly and cheerfully; above all, never admitting the possibility of defeat.

Next to self-control a sense of humour is the most tremendous help to us in every way in the bringing up of children, and is especially needed if we are apt to be impatient.

Besides love and patience we must show great *firmness*. A constant watch should be kept against slackness, and an endless fight against the self-indulgence and pleasure to ourselves of giving a child everything he wants or making life too easy for him. How can children learn to be unselfish, strong and self-controlled if all difficulties are smoothed out of their young lives for them by someone else, if every whim is gratified, if they are allowed to eat what they like, play when they like, and do not show consideration for other people. They will never respect us unless they see that we are strong and able to govern, and know what we say we *mean* and we insist upon.

Encourage, encourage, encourage. A few words of praise will do more to help him on the right way than ten thousand of blame. Encouragement cures diffidence and gives self-confidence. We must let our children know that we have immense faith in them, and expect much from them as they grow up – then they will have a high standard to live up to.

That *explanation* is a very obvious necessity in the upbringing of a reasoning being is proved by the endless questions children ask, but one that often, through thoughtlessness or laziness, we neglect. We tell children not to do or say a certain thing; we say that it is 'naughty' and we are too impatient to explain why. A little talk to point out the opposite path, and why that is to be desired, impresses the right upon them and not the wrong, and sends their curiosity flying in that direction, so that they will think about it and ask questions until they understand.

When children are small the little things should be explained to them as well as the big. As they grow older, it is wiser to put the facts before them and to encourage them to draw their own conclusions so that they learn to think for themselves.

THE FOUR GREAT BODILY NECESSITIES

From the moment of birth onward there are four great bodily necessities, which depend neither on a well-filled purse nor on a luxurious home, but which are in everyone's power.

The first great need is *Air*, fresh, clean, outdoor air. We can exist for three weeks without food, for three days without water, but not for three minutes without air. We cannot always be taking our children out of doors, but fresh air can always be taken in to them. Our first care must be to open the windows; our next, to keep them open. Bedding needs fresh air, as well as the bedroom; the larder, as well as the living room.

The second essential is *Light*. We cannot always ensure a sunny aspect for our children's rooms, though we should always try to do so, but we can at least refrain from considering carpets and curtains before the children's well-being, and from blocking out the light we can get by filling up the valuable window space with toilet-tables, by overcrowding our rooms with furniture, and by neglecting to have our windows regularly cleaned.

Exercise can prevent and can cure many of the ills to which our flesh is heir, but should never be allowed while the process of digestion is at its height, or when the system is depressed through fatigue or fasting.

Rest is just as essential to health as exercise. In these hurrying, bustling days it is especially important to insist on children having a) the rest of proper leisure by day, and b) the rest of proper sleep by night. Children must not be chivvied through life with their every moment mapped out for them on time-tables. Leisure is needed, in which we can discover, and they can follow, their individual bent, or have that thorough relaxation which is often their best recreation.

Rest must be really restful, and it must be taken under good and sanitary conditions, viz., a) in separate beds, and airy rooms; b) in healthy and decent attitudes; c) with warm, but light coverings; d) with stomachs neither replete, nor empty; and e) with freedom from night-terrors and from troubled consciences.

A FEW RULES TO BEGIN WITH

Be patient.

Do not expect great improvement all at once.

Do not hurry a child more than necessary.

Be firm. When you decide on a thing, stick to it, and see it through.

Be consistent. If you disapprove of a thing one day, disapprove of it the next.

Be calm. Do not frighten, excite or upset your child any more than you can help.

Pay as much attention to good behaviour as to bad behaviour.

Ask yourself why you are interfering. Never interfere without good reason.

When you prevent a baby or young child from doing something, give him an alternative outlet.

Give a young child a few minutes' warning of a demand.

Wherever possible give a positive order rather than a negative one.

Say 'do this' rather than 'do not do that'.

Give an alternative wherever possible. 'Stay here and be quiet or go into the other room to make that noise.'

Encourage the child to do everything that he can for himself.

Allow the child to make his own choice wherever possible.

Do not talk about a child in front of him.

Do not ridicule or disparage a child.

Be as polite and considerate to your child as you would he should be to you.

If possible control your voice tones. A cross tone of voice invariably brings a cross and negative reaction from the child.

Avoid arousing very strong emotion, especially shame, fear or hate.

Do not read an adult meaning into a childish action.

II

GOOD — AND BAD — BEHAVIOUR

ENCOURAGING GOOD BEHAVIOUR

THE more we get into the habit of regarding a child as a person with the same desires and emotions as ourselves, the more easily we will learn to understand her and to manage her.

Children do what we say in the first place because they want to please us and for us to love them. If our requests are always reasonable, not too frequent or frustrating, they will do what we say because they know that we would not insist if we do not have a good reason.

Discipline is necessary but it should never be used for its own sake.

Children do silly, inconvenient, stupid things, but they rarely do wicked things. We should make them understand the silliness of their acts and the inconvenience or pain that they have caused. We should explain how best they can clear up the mess, comfort the pain or make up for their stupidity, but we should never let them feel that by their actions they have lost our confidence.

The child takes over by suggestion, not only the actions, but *the emotional moods and feelings of the parents.* To treat a child unjustly not merely makes her resentful and gives her a sense of injustice, it will make her unjust. Always bring to bear on the child the mood you want to induce in the child.

Do not make the strain of obedience too great. That is, try in some degree to protect the child from the temptation she finds hard to resist. If, for instance, you know that the sugar basin has special temptation for some little child, do not leave it in an accessible place.

In giving orders or direction to a child, let

them be *affirmative*, not *negative*, e.g. 'Now you will carry that carefully', not 'Now mind you don't drop that'. In this way you make her believe in herself, and give her confidence in the undertaking.

When a child has done something not quite rightly or well, you will help her much more if you blame the fault rather than the child. When Alice comes in with muddy boots, say, 'Oh, Alice, look at all that mud. It is not nice on the carpet!' rather than, 'Oh, Alice, you're a bad girl to bring so much mud on to my carpet!'

If it is your pleasant duty to give praise, praise the effort rather than the achievement, and the thing done rather than the child doing it.

SAYING 'NO' AND 'DON'T'

It is never too early to begin a child's moral education. A parent who begins such training only when they cannot shut their eyes to the fact that their child is greedy, disobedient and gives way to temper whenever she is contradicted, has lost ground with her which it may take them years to make up, if they ever succeed in doing so.

Perhaps one of the greatest mistakes a mother can make is being afraid to use the word 'No', and, on the other hand, being prodigal of the word 'Don't'. The word 'don't' should be expunged from the vocabulary because it is simply repressive. It is not final like 'No', and therefore a quick child will perpetually return to the charge, the mother gets weary of resisting it, and the former at last gains an easy victory.

Nagging is about the worst course we can adopt; and if we think we are being firm by saying 'don't' about most things and noticing every little fault and mistake, we are the mistaken ones ourselves. The secret is to concentrate on the big things, and to distinguish between the passing tricks of childhood and those habits which will endure or harm their characters.

It depends very much on a child's temperament whether she becomes too submissive or aggressive and we should adapt our handling accordingly. We should try not to rub small children the wrong way any more than we can help, but with the best will in the world temper storms will occur. As well as being prevented by us from doing the things she wants to do, she will be prevented from doing other things by her own lack of strength and skill, and she will relieve her frustration by a discharge of anger.

Some tantrums can be very severe. The child will not only scream, she will bite and scratch, stamp and kick and even bang her head on the wall or floor. It is essential on these occasions that we should keep calm. The child should not be left to scream herself into a state of complete exhaustion, and she should be restrained from hurting us and from hurting herself. By holding her gently but firmly and remaining unruffled by her rage, we can help her to regain control.

Take no notice of an ordinary display of temper. If the noise is excessive, we can say quite pleasantly, 'I don't like that noise; if you want to make it, please make it in the other room', and lead her there and shut the door.

A child should never achieve her aims by a temper display but neither should she be punished. It is a natural stage in her growth and we can best help her by setting her a good example and showing her patience and understanding. If tears and temper never get her her own way, she will soon outgrow them.

The spoilt child will resent a tightening of discipline and there will be periods of tears during which the indulgent parent must harden his heart. The frustrated child will be bewildered by the lack of interference and for a few days may exploit the situation by behaving more wildly and more aggressively than ever. This is a natural compensatory move and we should leave it to take its course, unless she is hurting us or our possessions or herself.

There are varying kinds of 'naughtiness' in growing children which are apt to unduly worry the anxious parent. But for peace of mind, she should always remember that exuberance which expresses itself in mischief is not, necessarily, something to worry about.

The mischievous child is the healthy child.

If you find the child employed in some mischief which you feel *should* be corrected, the surest way of putting an end to it is to pretend to be *interested* in the child's mischievous plan of action, thus showing that it isn't quite the wicked thing the child had imagined it to be.

Do not reprove your child before other people if you would develop in her a feeling of self-respect. If her self-respect is gone you will never be able to make her take pride in her behaviour.

If your child is stubborn, try changing her mind through suggestion before you resort to force. It will work in most cases if she doesn't realize what you are doing, and when the habit

is once broken she can be reasoned with and your trouble is practically over.

You should never let her know that you consider her hard to manage. Make her feel that your word is law finally and that you don't think for a moment that it will be disobeyed.

Do not on any account resort to bribery in the management of children. A sweet, a cake or a promise of money may, apparently, be the easiest way to appeal to them, but it is disastrous to the character, and encourages the appetites and baser desires.

LYING AND STEALING

Children may lie because they are afraid, or romancing, or to get some fancied advantage, but the usual reason they lie is because they are lied to.

If you would have your child grow up to be truthful, *never tell her a falsehood*. The little white lies told to acquaintances make an impression on a child's mind and she cannot differentiate between them and a really harmful lie.

Keeping one attitude for the home and another for the outside world is also sure to breed insincerity. Even politeness may be a dangerous thing to teach if it is made too artificial.

Children should never be accused of lying unless it is positively proved.

A feeling for ownership – a respect for property rights, if developed in very early childhood, may usually be trusted to persist through life. Yet in too many homes there is no rigid division of property so that children have no sense of mine and thine. Handkerchiefs, stockings, toys, are regarded as common property and borrowed without formality. Children who grow up in this kind of atmosphere are not likely to be scrupulous later if confronted by temptation.

WRONGS AND PUNISHMENTS

Never make a *threat* to a child that you do not carry out, even if you repent having threatened her. Simply be more careful next time to decide how far you should go with a threat before you utter it.

If a child has done wrong, look for the cause of the trouble and try substituting desirable activities for those to be corrected.

Some preaching we must do, and a little of it may be effective. 'This is right', 'That is wrong', we tell our children, and possibly sometimes they heed us and save themselves some pains.

If a child has not been made insensitive by rough treatment, she is quite sufficiently disciplined by the disapproving or distressed attitude of those she loves, and will grieve most wholesomely until favour is restored.

Isolation is a severe and perfectly logical punishment. It is not wise to put a child to bed in the day time, but it is often wise to keep her for a brief time in a room by herself, 'to think it over', and it is sometimes very wise, though it takes fortitude, to keep her home (under supervision) from the anticipated party or picnic.

III

SPEAKING AND LISTENING

QUESTIONS AND ANSWERS

A child ought to ask questions. Some parents find this period tiresome, but it is all-important to the child's development. It is his main method of learning and we should always answer him to the best of our ability. If we do not know the answer we should say so and try to find out from a book or from someone who knows.

When we know that the child knows the answer himself we should say, 'You tell me.' Wherever possible in explaining how something works let the child do it for himself or show him slowly how we do it.

Never tell a child that he is too young to understand. He would not ask the question unless he had reached the age of wanting to know.

Some children ask more questions than others, but it is only the child who has been put off with an inadequate answer or no answer at all who will keep on asking the same question.

It is wiser not to show embarrassment, shock or anger at the things our children say or at the questions they ask us. If we do they will go elsewhere for their information.

If a child is clamouring for your attention, always insist that he shall 'keep quiet for a minute' before you hear what he has to say. There is, however, one danger in this system, illustrated by the story of King Edward VII, who first ate the caterpillar in his salad, and then turned to listen to his grandson's warning interruption.

The good-mannered child should answer when spoken to and should never 'answer back'.

It is sometimes difficult to gauge the child's ability to comprehend what he hears others say. We should always make sure that the child grasps what we are telling him – get his attention to begin with, and give him time to 'take it in'.

Sarcasm should never be used on young children: it is cruel and merely bewilders and alienates them. And teasing must be very sparingly employed. Young children take life very seriously, and by them teasing is usually misunderstood.

Real humour is quite another thing, and should be encouraged. Family jokes are invaluable; and wholesome wit and 'leg-pulling' is all to the good. The child who can see jokes even against themselves, and makes them too, rarely sulks.

Neither do we show our respect for our children by comparing them in their presence, or by quoting the virtues of one child to another. Such remarks are an insult and

injury both to the child addressed and the one spoken of, and serve no good purpose.

A child should not interrupt, but neither should he be ruthlessly interrupted. The little boy who complained 'Daddy scolds me for interrupting him, but when I just looked at him for interrupting me he sent me from the table', had justice on his side.

CHILDREN'S SPEECH AND LANGUAGE

Pains should be taken with the youngest children to make them enunciate well.

Insist that children do not talk all at once, at least in the company of grown-ups, or call back and forth from room to room.

Running words together, in a youknow-whatImean manner is generally the result of impatience and an excess of nervous energy. Speak slowly and distinctly to the child and give them time to finish what they have to say.

Unfinished sentences are usually due to sloppy thinking and lack of concentration.

Insist on the child's finishing one thought before they start another.

Mumbling and thick, indistinct speech may result from shyness or be just lazy articulation. Always try to speak very distinctly to the child.

Numbers of people pronounce their words well yet possess vocabularies which are poor beyond description. Little children ought to be read to from the very first. So will they quite naturally become the possessors of a wide vocabulary, and for each circumstance of life have fit words in which to express themselves and their ideas.

IV

CERTAIN PRINCIPLES

THE chief quality required in arranging children's food is common sense.

The simpler the food the better. Pickles, sauces, tea, coffee and other sophisticated stimulants should be avoided, as should also rich food like pork, duck and goose.

Variety is essential.

No 'pieces' of any description should be given between meals.

Three meals a day for a normal child over one year are ample.

If a child does not seem hungry, leave her alone; missing a meal will do her no harm.

See that the child has plenty of fresh green vegetables and fruit during the day, and water to drink between meals. The mere provision of the vegetable, curiously enough, is not sufficient: it must be actually eaten.

Insist on thorough mastication. Do not mince up all meat as though the child were toothless. Sit by her and show her how to bite.

Avoid the frequent use of sweet biscuits. The ordinary shop biscuits have practically no nutritive value, but, because they are very little trouble, they are often given indiscriminately to children.

The question of chocolates and similar sweets is a very difficult one. They are undoubtedly bad for the teeth, but if your children are not to be isolated from all others it is difficult and perhaps hardly necessary to forbid them altogether. If, however, you must give them sweets, give them at meal-times. It is the incessant chewing of sweets that does the harm.

Do not provide large quantities of sweets and cakes to be eaten on a journey. The only sensible plan on a long journey is to keep as closely as possible to the children's usual meal-times, to choose plain food to which they are accustomed, and to give no extras.

Do not let the taking of sugar become mechanical. Insist that a pudding should be tasted before it is sprinkled with sugar.

The same remarks apply equally to salt. Do not let it be eaten recklessly. It is unnecessary to add it to a very young child's food at table; a sufficient quantity should be used in the cooking, but the child should be given it when she asks for it, not before, and be taught to put it at the side of her plate and to dip her food into it like a human being.

Do not follow the common practice of describing everything forbidden as 'nasty'. What must a child think of a mother who describes as 'nasty' a plate of, e.g. strawberries, which everyone, including herself, is eating with evident enjoyment? Surely it is better to say simply: 'You shall have it when you are bigger'?

When your child asks at the end of a meal for some delicacy which you intend to refuse, do not offer her a stone in the form of a piece of dry bread. The statement, 'If you could eat another meringue, you can eat this bread', is so obviously untrue that the child merely puts you down as one lacking in understanding; as indeed you are.

The question of likes and dislikes is not an easy one. Tastes in food should never be discussed when children are present. Her food should be put before her with no comment and it should be taken for granted that she will eat it. She will almost invariably do what is expected of her.

If a child does not finish what is put before her, do not 'make a song' about it. Say, 'You're being rather silly, aren't you?' and leave it at that; but do not discuss it then or later, or substitute something else, or you will be encouraging her to wonder continually whether there is not something else that she would prefer to what is in front of her. See to it that the kind of food that has proved obnoxious is not offered again, but do *not* let her think that her expressed dislike has influenced you.

Resistance to food may be overcome in various ways. Withholding some desired tidbit until the spinach or carrots are eaten is often effective.

Avoid any attempt to persuade her to eat in order to deprive someone else of the food. This is a very usual mistake, and takes several forms, from 'I shall give it to Dolly; *she* likes it', to 'I shall give it to a poor little boy in the road.' What a lesson to teach the child! The legitimate method is very different: 'Dolly's hungry; let's give her some too.'

Try to avoid coaxing measures. If, in the presence of the child, you adopt a 'take-it-for-granted' attitude, and appear to assume that she will eat her food, she will – providing there is nothing seriously wrong with her – come to your way of thinking. Even 'tempers' and moods cannot resist, indefinitely, the call of hunger!

It is wiser not to call attention to new food but to serve it in the ordinary way with no special comment. If the child does not like the colour, shape or consistency and refuses a proffered spoonful, take it away and try it again in a few days' time.

Beware of engaging the infant in a struggle.

She is almost certain to win. All we have gained is an ugly scene.

TABLE MANNERS

It is a joy and pleasure to watch any child at meal-time who has been taught to be careful and neat in the way she eats her food, who does not make a noise with her mouth or speak when it is full. On the other hand, it is disgusting to have to sit at table with children who disregard these details.

Bad habits of eating are readily acquired but difficult to break.

See that children have their meals at proper times, and that they have proper time for their meals. We must wage war against the modern habit of 'feeding' rather than eating; food is shovelled in, and swallowed down, but because of this unseemly haste it is neither masticated nor digested as it should be.

When the child is old enough to understand, she should be served in her proper turn – last.

Nothing is worse training than to allow her to clamour until she is helped.

Young children should not be allowed to play with their food, nor should the habit be formed of amusing or diverting them while eating, because by these means more food is taken.

If orange spoons, butter knives, and the other pieces of silver used for convenience rather than necessity, are in common use at home, a child is never awkward when out in company.

Children do not respond readily to table etiquette. If parents will pretend they are visiting the children and will create an atmosphere of courtesy by being extremely courteous to each other and to the children, the children will enjoy the playfulness of it and sooner or later the habit of courtesy will be formed.

V

MANNERS AND COURTESY

GOOD manners are not the result of arbitrary rules which have been chosen haphazardly: they are the outcome of consideration for others which past generations have discovered; they are the outward and visible signs of a good heart which has been trained to regard the small conventions of life as well as the bigger issues, and they make the world an easier and pleasanter place to live in.

Young children often forget their 'manners' because they are overcome with shyness or pleasure. They are too shy to say 'hello' or 'goodbye', too overcome with pleasure to say 'thank you'. We should not scold them or press them to use the conventional phrase. When they are older they will be just as polite as the small child who can repeat all the right phrases. We are inclined to set our standards too high in this with the result that we often get a mechanical response and a rather grudging politeness.

It is much more difficult to train some children than others but it is imperative that we persist.

The small details of good manners are quickly learnt, and soon become good habits which we shall never forget, making us much more agreeable companions than we ever would be otherwise. No one likes to have bad-mannered people or children about.

Politeness begins at home. All the good manners which are right when we are with strangers are as necessary in the home.

The child in the home is the most representative example of the human 'counterfeit'. Parents are sometimes apt to forget this. If a mother is terse or rude to her husband in the presence of her children, it is not unnatural that the children should decide they have every right to be terse or rude to their parents. If a father's tendency to be captious and ungallant is exhibited in the presence of his children, the children are more likely than not to imitate this form of behaviour, and to resent being reprimanded for it!

Manners start in the cradle.

Even by eighteen months, always 'handing round' chocolates before helping himself should have been acquired. A baby of a year can easily be taught to put his hand in front of his mouth when he coughs.

'Thank you' and 'please' are simple words. They are easily learned by the smallest child.

All children should be taught to shake hands with a real grip and at the same time to look straight in the eyes of the person so greeted. A child flabbily offering a limp hand while gazing in the opposite direction is a frequent but unattractive spectacle.

When other children come to tea, great stress should be laid, before their arrival, on the fact that though the toys must, of course, be at the guests' service while they are in the house, they will without fail be left behind when they depart.

VI

CLEANLINESS, HEALTH AND SLEEP

GOOD GROOMING

HABITS formed in childhood have an everlasting influence. Habits of cleanliness when a child is small will bear their imprint, while habits of indolence and sloth in a parent will create a like tendency in the child.

As soon as the child is capable of understanding the meaning of words, and even sooner than that, with the aid of actions, she should be *trained*.

She can be told how to put her clothes away tidily when she undresses.

She can be shown to dispose of her various little toilet accessories – where to put her toothbrush, where to hang her towel, where to place her brush and comb.

The most successful way of training children to this appreciation of everyday routine and good habits is for the mother herself to take a pride in them. If a child sees that she pleases her mother by doing this or that thing in the right way, she is going to do it; it is so much *easier* for her!

The earlier the habits are formed, the easier the job – and the more effective the habits. The child who fusses about using a nail-brush when the dirt under her nails comes to parental attention, may be taught to take the regular use of the same brush with equanimity.

It is easier to establish these scheduled habits if the child has the proper tools to work with. And the results are sure to be better. See that your child has toothbrushes adapted to her mouth and with bright handles. See that she has a little brightly coloured nail-brush, a hair-brush that fits her hand and is not too heavy for her to wield herself. A comb that is easy to manage, a mirror in which she can see herself.

The rod for her towels and flannel should be within reach. The towels themselves should be of distinctive colour so that she does not confuse them with the towels of others.

POSTURE

Keep an eye on your child's posture from the very beginning. When she sits, see that she sits well back in her chair with chest up and back straight. When she walks, see that she places her feet parallel and walks with abdomen in and chest up.

The proper height in tables and chairs is of great importance in giving children correct posture habits. Feet that don't reach the floor and tables too low for the chairs are distinct impediments.

As children lengthen out and perhaps get a little self-conscious, sometimes they begin to slouch. Don't let this tendency develop.

As the child grows older, you can also depend on well-directed games and sports to help develop figure and posture. Swimming builds long muscles, develops high chests, and slim hips and abdomen, skating and dancing poise and grace. Riding develops muscular control, especially in the abdomen.

A child who attends a dancing class is not going to fall awkwardly over chairs and rugs when she reaches *the awkward age*.

TEETH AND TEETHING

It is impossible to take too much care of the teeth, for toothache is among the least of the evils caused by neglect.

The teeth should be cleaned twice a day, morning and evening.

Nothing bad enough can be said of the habit of 'tucking a child up with a chocolate'. 'Medicine after she is in bed' is another pernicious custom. It cannot be said too often or too emphatically that *nothing whatever should be put into the mouth at night after the tooth-brush* except a drink of water.

The actual cleaning should be a careful process; it should be made into a game to enlist the child's interest (e.g., the operator and the child should both sing 'Ah!' thus keeping the mouth well open).

All children should be taken regularly to a good dentist. Warn the household not to frighten the child about the proposed visit. It is pointless to make her suffer days of frightened anticipation.

BEDTIME AND SLEEP

One of our greatest crimes against the child in these whirling times is in failing to see that she has sufficient rest. We take unjustifiable liberties with the regular nap time and early bedtime that sometimes interfere with adult projects.

Disturbed sleep or sleeplessness may be acquired by faulty training; as when the nursery is lighted and the child taken from her crib whenever she wakes or cries.

Any excitement or romping play just before bedtime, and fears aroused by pictures or stories, are frequent causes. There may be physical discomfort from cold feet, insufficient or too much clothing, or want of fresh air in the sleeping room.

Every child should have a bed to herself and if possible a room to herself – a space of her own where she can keep her own possessions and be by herself at times.

Children are naturally averse to being put to sleep and will do all they can to make it difficult. They will think of endless excuses for putting it off.

One happy method of inducing a child to go to bed was discovered by one ingenious mother. A child was told at night that she would find certain toys under her bed the next day and if she went to bed willingly she would receive her favourite toys but if a fuss was made, she would have to take whatever she could get. She was always willing to go to bed and eager to get up, for the day was to hold something of a surprise.

WHEN THEY'RE ILL

All efforts should be made to prevent illness. Children who are coddled in hot rooms are far more susceptible to every kind of infection than those whose systems are braced by plenty of cold air.

Remember that 'hardening' children does not mean leaving their heads uncovered in a broiling sun, running about without dressing-gown and slippers after hot baths. Nor is it coddling to see that their feet are kept dry and warm, and that on a particularly cold day they wear an extra-warm coat.

When a child is ill nothing can be worse for her than outspoken pity: 'Poor dear, doesn't she look bad!' and the child droops at once, partly unconsciously and partly to gain sympathy, instead of trying to be plucky and make the best of things.

With a very small child stress can be laid *not* on the fact that she is ill, but on the fact that she is in bed for a treat, with special toys, etc. Relays of pictures can be fastened to the walls, and many little surprises can be arranged, such as curiously coloured puddings, fish, etc.

An 'Asleep' notice fastened to the door is invaluable during rest times, and so is a soft towel twisted tightly round both handles to hold the latch back, so that the door can be noiselessly opened and shut.

It will be a great help to the doctor if the child has been taught to show her tongue. A child should not connect this with ill-health, the formula being, 'Let's have a look at your tongue to see if it's grown.' Gargling is another useful accomplishment and can also be taught as a game.

When unpleasant medicine has to be given it is unwise to tell the child that it is 'nice'. You may get one dose down by this means, but the chances are that there will be a scene over the next, and, what is far worse, the child may afterwards distrust your word. It is far better to say something like this: 'This isn't very nice, but I want you to take it, so see how quickly you can drink it and how brave you can be.'

VII

SOME GENERAL GUIDANCE

THE main purpose in selecting a child's clothing should be not style nor beauty primarily, but the comfort and convenience of the child.

Sometimes the nursery-school children seem obsessed by the fear of injuring their clothing. While it may be proper to check undue destructiveness or wanton carelessness, it is certainly unfortunate to give children a disproportionate respect for material things. It is better to provide coarser garments and more of them than to check wholesome play or permit unnecessary worry.

To *keep* children clean is something that should never be attempted. It cannot be done and yet have them normal, healthy children. A child is not less attractive because he isn't fresh, but an accumulation of yesterday's dirt is most repulsive.

See to it that dressing is as little of an ordeal as may be, and that they learn as soon as possible to dress themselves.

Children's clothing should be suitable to the season. On the whole there is more danger of dressing children too warmly rather than not warmly enough, particularly in winter in our overheated houses.

Great care should be taken to see that all clothing is loose and comfortable, with no pressure, rubbing or irritation.

The temptation to 'dress up' children for the pleasure of adults should be sternly resisted.

If the children are taught to put away their hats and coats immediately upon coming in, you will be saved time and temper in the long run.

VIII

PARENTS AND PLAYTIME

THE problem of what to do with healthy children at home, when they are not asleep and dreaming, is one of some magnitude. It is wise to have a plan of action if the parents hope to get any peace and to be free of the perpetual anxiety about the safety of children which attends leaving them to their own devices.

Ideally, of course, a playroom especially furnished to minimize risk of accidents is the best solution to the problem. The next best thing is to choose a large corner of the room you can best afford to leave in a state of perpetual chaos.

The children's playtime should be free of petty restrictions, and their natural exuberance and creative instincts should be given every chance to flourish.

Whatever the natural preference of a child may prove to be, it should be encouraged, not discouraged. Even if you feel, at times, that a child is devoting an inordinate amount of time and energy to the indulgence of a pet hobby or game, excluding all other forms of amusement, it is not wise to discourage the habit. Don't, therefore, let any carping little doubt worry you about the advisibility of letting your child indulge her interest in a particular hobby or game. The rest of her little brain is not rusting because she uses so much of it, apparently, in the cause of her favourite pastime.

A parent should never play down to a child, but should always put himself on an equal basis. He is one of them at this time and if he wishes to make himself popular with the children, he must forget for the time being that he is anything more than a child with them.

When the children are unduly noisy, it only means an abundance of animal spirits and they should be permitted to work them off in some way. If there is plenty of outdoors, the problem is solved and they should get out and run – race, if they want to. For the indoor child, the problem is greater, but if there is a chance for gymnasium work, callisthenics, or even room enough for somersaults, the child can be satisfied.

Respect the concentration of children and do not thoughtlessly interrupt serious occupations. How often a little child, busily engaged in some undertaking, be it a building of bricks or making a mud pie, is suddenly seized upon, bundled up and hustled off to the much more important *next thing*. If the *next thing* is *really* important (a walk, or dinner or something of that kind) give due warning.

The educational value of pets is enormous, but we must be sure to see for ourselves that the child is quite regular in feeding the animals, and cleaning their house and cages.

Do not discourage friendships simply because you do not happen to feel *personally* drawn towards the subject of your child's choice.

The pleasures and benefits gained usually far outweigh the disadvantages. Habits, speech or mannerisms picked up in this way are not lasting, although they may be annoying to us at the time.

Discourage them, by all means, when you feel instinctively that they can do no good, and may do harm; but even in such a case as this, it will be best to use tact and patience. There is no more sure way of alienating a child's affections than by assuming a dictatorial attitude in relation to the personal preferences of a child.

Cultivate your children's friends. They have a very powerful influence and you will find that to make friends of the children you want for your child's playmates will be a great power in influencing her against those whose influence is unwholesome.

Children should always have someone

young enough to romp with, and they should be taught not to shriek, and not to hit out wildly, and they should also learn to stop instantly on the word of their parents.

Children happily at play should be left to themselves.

Have them play within sight and hearing but do not make yourself too evident. An adult should be resorted to only as a court of last appeal when the children cannot settle their differences among themselves.

Games of chance and skill will do more toward developing honesty and fairness in the child than all the preaching that can be given them, for their games take the place of business battles later in life. A child must either play fair with the other children or get out. They will not tolerate dishonesty.

If a parent discovers that a child peeks when he is supposed to be hiding his eyes, something should be done and done at once. It should never, under any circumstances, pass by unnoticed.

Many little children are made miserable by extreme shyness. If mothers would make a point of occasionally leaving children in charge of others and bringing company into the home more frequently, children would not developing this agonizing shyness, which too often persists into maturity and robs human intercourse of half its pleasure.

Another less common way of withdrawing from the group, harder to understand and deal with, is the unsocial attitude of the child who appears averse to joining the group because she is sufficient unto herself rather than shy. Experience seems to indicate that this trait is found only in children who can do things better than the others and would rather play alone than be annoyed by the stupidity of their neighbours. It requires extremely careful handling.

These children should not be forced into the group, but every effort should be made to find them friends who can give them real companionship as well as what points of congeniality with the general group are possible. Often the natures that are unable to be 'good mixers', that are unhappy trying to be 'one of the bunch', have valuable contributions to make. They should not be embittered or discouraged by having their differences regarded as a disadvantage but should be given as much companionship as they desire and as much letting alone.

TOYS

Choose safe and colourful toys for the very young baby.

Insist on hygiene in the playroom; infection is so easily carried by the dirt and grime which is allowed to collect on toys, books and such things.

When baby reaches toddling age, encourage toys which help her physical development. Cars which can be pushed about the floor; rocking-horses and chairs and such like toys to help develop the muscles.

Whenever possible let the child make his own toys. He will much prefer walnut shell boats with a match for mast that he has helped to make, to the most expensive clockwork model bought in a shop.

You will be wise, too, if from the moment your baby is born you begin collecting pictures for scrap books and 'cutting out'.

Handwork hobbies should, whenever possible, be encouraged. Most children will develop an interest in crayons, or paints, or cardboard figure-building, and such quiet games give them the rest they sometimes need from the more vigorous and active forms of play.

A child should always put away her own toys, and she should know that she is to do it before she eats or before she goes to bed.

The growing child can be trained, without realizing the process, to a habit of tidiness by the simple ruse of giving her territorial rights in the playroom. A little box that shuts up and locks up, with a specially reserved place for the storing of the key, will give a child a sense of importance and responsibility. All the toys, when finished with for the day, go into the box.

Books should always be treated with the very greatest care.

There is no need whatever to let a baby handle papers of any kind until she is old enough to treat them gently. Washable books are always available, and the kind printed on boards.

Besides the tearing of books, scribbling in them should also be absolutely prohibited. If the child has been allowed to scribble in cheap books, how can she understand where the line is drawn?

Do not let your child read trash or look at inferior pictures merely because they are given to her; they will vitiate her taste. The ideal plan is to go through everything yourself first. Terrifying images are to be found in nursery books to an inexplicable extent.

Do not let the child, at any age, feel that she is bound by rules as to what she reads. The chief effect of this is to make the forbidden books attractive. If a supply of suitable books is always at hand, and objectionable ones are kept out of the way, there should be no need for rules. It is fatal to take a book away when it is half-read, as the incident will merely impress it on the mind.

Do not answer breathless enquiries such as 'Does he get there in time?' It spoils the literary value of the story, and leads to the bad habits of skipping and 'looking at the end of the book first'. The exception to this is, of course, the reassurance of an obviously scared child.

Do not be over-anxious about the book-worm child. Any reading is better than no reading, for it at least indicates that the child is willing and anxious to make discoveries and explore new fields. To discourage a child from reading is foolish; to see that she reads in a good light, so that the eyes cannot be hurt, is wise.

One helpful way of inculcating a love of good and healthy books in the child who *will* read whenever she gets a chance, is to encourage the collection by her of a personal library. Buy books for birthdays and other festive gift-times; inscribe the books to her, to give them the personal touch, and encourage the safeguarding of the books so that she grows to consider them as a sacred charge.

IN THE GARDEN AND OUT-OF-DOORS

Whenever it is possible, give a child a bit of garden to do just what she likes with, to plan, to dig, and to plant her own flowers in. She will have much more interest in the thing she makes for herself and feels is really her own to do what she likes with.

Let the child do what she will with her own 'estate'.

Help, when you feel that your help will be acceptable, with the choice of plants and seeds and, no matter what kind of a 'bungle' she makes of the job, keep on appearing to be interested in the growth and destiny of that all-important corner.

Every mother is not fortunate in having a garden into which she can put her children in the sunny, warm hours of the day. But the open spaces, commons and parks are available to all.

IX

CHILDREN'S PARTY-GIVING

GIVING A PARTY

Most parents regard it as a social duty to give two or more children's parties every year – a duty which would be all pleasure, were it not for the work and worry which the giving of a really successful party usually entails.

What is it, then, which creates the glamour of a party? Probably a number of factors contribute towards it but perhaps, more than anything else, the feeling, which all children share, that they are persons of importance and *all this is being done for them.*

The most successful party will be the one where the organizer knows how to provide something *different* in games and entertainments, or to give these a fresh and original turn.

Every detail should be thought out ahead, from the sending of invitations – intended to arouse pleasure in anticipation – to the preparing of a list of games and entertainments, so that there may be no dull moments of 'wondering what to play next'. Any necessary music must be arranged for; decorations for rooms and tables planned with care; and refreshments provided, which are not only attractive, but also suited to young digestions. Perhaps a special 'stunt', or a surprise, which will make the party a memorable event for many weeks and days to come, will figure on the programme.

Party-giving should not be regarded as a social duty only – a mere return of hospitality received. The real essence of a party is *to give the children a thoroughly good time.*

All the children invited to a party should be, as far as possible, of a similar age. In the case of a family where there are children of widely differing ages, it is a far better plan to give two parties, one for the older children and another for the little ones, on two separate days, rather than one party for all of them together. A good organizer will probably arrange for these two parties to be given on consecutive days, which will greatly simplify the catering.

LET THE CHILDREN HELP

Party-giving provides an opportunity for teaching children to think, to organize and to plan for the entertainment of others.

Most parents are in the habit of giving parties '*for* their children', and instead of being the hosts with duties to carry out, the young people are generally no more than *guests*. Let the children give their own parties! The arrangements, such as making lists of games, planning competitions and other entertainments, provide engrossing occupations for long winter afternoons. Even the youngest can take a share in the planning.

The first question will be, 'Whom shall we invite?' The children should learn to remember their friends and make their own lists of guests. From these lists the actual children to be invited can afterwards be chosen – and it may require considerable tact to find reasons why some of the proposed guests should not be included!

Then comes the duty of sending out the invitations. Those children who are old enough to write should do this themselves as far as possible.

Games and entertainments should also be suggested by the children. Those who are old enough may prepare lists of all the jolly games they know – lists which mother and father can afterwards edit and amplify. The final list should consist of quiet and noisy games alternating.

Children should be taught at an early age to entertain their visitors instead of expecting *to be entertained.*

TINY TOTS

All small children are familiar with their nursery rhymes, and so, many pretty games may be devised around these. They are particularly charming when played to music. Take for instance, the well-known rhyme 'Hey diddle diddle/The Cat and the Fiddle'. First let all the children sing it together whilst dancing around in a ring; then allocate a part to each of the little ones. Another way of playing these games is to give to each child a picture of the character he is supposed to represent.

A Tiny Tots' garden party may take the form of a 'flower party', each of the little ones being dressed as a flower. Besides playing games, the children will indulge in such competitions as making posies, daisy chains and wreaths of leaves.

GAMES AND SPORTS

Children's games fall roughly under two headings – quiet games and noisy games. The noisy ones with plenty of movement are always popular, especially with the younger children; quiet games are more suitable for the older girls and boys. Noisy games include: Blind Man's Buff, ball games, hide and seek, kiss in the ring, musical chairs, oranges and lemons. Garden games include: ball games, hide and seek, races and sports, gardener and scamps, cat and mouse. Quiet games include: guessing games, forfeits, paper and pencil games, postman's knock, whistle game.

Competitive sports are usually the principal event of an outdoor party, but they often degenerate into an unorganized scramble.

There should be at least two organizers – a starter and a judge. The space dedicated to the races must be kept completely clear, and if there is no natural boundary line, a rope should be stretched along the lawn or a piece of tape fastened down on each side. An ordinary step-ladder or some other elevation must be provided for the judge so that he may sit in state and get a clear bird's-eye view over the whole course. The starter must have a whistle, and the judge should be provided with a notebook in which to set down the winners of each event. Handicaps may be given for age or physical discrepancies.

The list suggested here makes quite a useful programme: flat racing; obstacle races; three-legged race; four-legged race (with hands and feet touching the ground); spoon race; jumping contests; sack race; hopping races.

PLANNING THE MENU

Good things to eat, attractively prepared and daintily served, are probably one of the greatest attractions of a children's party. While we generally aim to give them all that the heart – or, should we say the palate – of a child could possibly desire, some thought must be given to the morning after.

The formula should be – plain but attractive. When most of the items on the menu are home-made, then one can be certain that they contain only the choicest and most harmless of ingredients.

It is quite easy to make even the plainest food look attractive by the manner in which it is served. The simplest of sandwiches, by the judicious use of colourful fillings, may be as tempting as the savoury sandwiches on the tables of grown-up persons. The plainest of sponge cakes, with different coloured icings, are as attractive to look at as a dish of mille-feuilles and cream pastries; and they cannot harm the most gluttonous of kiddies.

DISTRIBUTING GIFTS

At many parties, especially at Christmas time, a feature is made of distributing gifts. The purchasing of gifts will naturally have to be undertaken by mother or father, for whilst the children have very strong ideas as to what their friend would like to have, they do not always realize that mother's purse and daddy's pocket are not infinite in depth!

When the collection of gifts has been purchased, the children can take a hand in allocating them; in wrapping them attractively; or in advising some special idea for their distribution – such as the arrival of the postman!

DANCES FOR YOUNG PEOPLE
For a large dance it is best to engage the services of a professional pianist, or even a small jazz band. For a small and more intimate party a plentiful supply of up-to-date dance records serves the purpose very well. In either case, the sequence of the dance music should be decided before the party.

There are many novel ways of choosing partners which provide lots of fun and entertainment. One way is to blindfold all the men, who must then try and catch a partner without seeing who she is. Another is to distribute short lengths of ribbon in different colours, one set being handed around amongst the boys, and a duplicate among the girls. A similar method is to prepare badges in couples: Jack and Jill; Bubble and Squeak; Fish and Chips; Romeo and Juliet; Dante and Beatrice; and so on.

A 'flirtation' dance is always popular and amusing, and is quite easy to arrange. Boys and girls pair off, and must then change partners quickly whenever the music stops.

Kiss and hiss is an amusing game if played as an interlude. The girls go outside the room, and the boys, who remain seated, each select a partner. Each girl comes in separately and must curtsey to the boy she thinks has chosen her. If her guess is correct he dances with her; if not, she is hissed and has to go out of the room again until the other girls have had their turn. The game can be reversed.

X

PREPARING THEM FOR A LIFE OF THEIR OWN

ADOLESCENCE

CHILDREN between the ages of ten and sixteen often appear to have inexplicable and, perhaps, rather disturbing whims and fancies. They veer this way and that in their interests; they get 'mopey' at some periods and over-exuberant at others.

This difficult phase of growth, both of mind and body, is vaguely disturbing to the child. The parent is able to help and sustain her children through this growing period, and through the years of adolescence, by a sane and healthy attitude towards them, and a willingness to share their little problems and, whenever possible, help to solve them.

In dealing with adolescents it is never wise to impose our will, to try to dominate the new generation. More is accomplished by indirect suggestion than by so-called advice, which is often a euphemism for nagging.

It is possible to over-value the quality of obedience. A certain amount of independence and arrogance is natural in healthy adolescence. Some measure of egoism, in adolescence especially, is inseparable from healthy ambition, the determination to make something of life.

We must be prepared to lose our children if we are to keep them. Let them feel free, untrammelled, at liberty. Let them know life through experience.

The child who has been brought up on the lines of self-discipline and self-control can be trusted with a latch-key in adolescence.

It is well to remember that it is impossible to restrain, to keep boys and girls 'good', obedient, loyal to their parents, except by love and trust. The adolescent will find opportunity for outwitting the most terrorizing disciplinarian, the most harsh of parents.

Some adolescents are afraid of grown-ups, others are intolerant of older people, and others again are hypercritical. To acquire the habit of regarding people hypercritically, unkindly, is fatal to happy living. A generous outlook, charity of thought, will make life easier and far more successful from every point of view.

Allow young people to have their pleasures in their own home and you will not lie awake night after night when they have reached an independent age wondering if they are in good company.

If young people have plenty of wholesome fun they are not going to seek harmful pleasures. Know where your children are and enter as much as possible into their pleasures. There is no surer way of gaining their confidence.

A knowledge of the virtues and the difference between right and wrong must be impressed on the inner consciousness, so that clear paths and strong centres are formed in the brain, and 'good habits' made.

We should tell them why they should be kind and self-controlled, patient, strong, courageous, truthful, honest and industrious, polite and good-mannered; have pure thoughts; protect the weak and unfortunate; love everyone in general, and parents, relatives and friends in particular; also that they should not eat too much or abuse their bodies in any way.

It is most important to develop the Conscience. The conscience does not decide what is a virtue or what is not, but it is the instinct within us, the 'still small voice', which urges us to do what we believe to be right and makes us uneasy and miserable when we have done wrong.

It is very wise to teach children the value of money and to let them have the use of a small allowance as soon as possible. It is also very good for them to be encouraged to save what they can from their allowances or any presents of money. This teaches them to save and gives them a feeling of self-respect and responsibility.

Gently restrain any tendency towards buying sweets. If they must buy anything to eat, fruit is better.

A good scheme is to encourage them to find or buy materials and make their own presents and toys.

HELPING AT HOME

Children who expect mother to do 'everything' grow eventually into children who take everything *out* of mother. Even if they do mess a job up, when they attempt to do it; even if mother knows it would be done more quickly and correctly by herself, it is not fair, either to the mother or her children, to relieve the children of every little task. If they are made to understand from the beginning that certain things are expected of them, they will automatically and quite happily do those things.

The parent who does not teach her child to perform certain household tasks regularly need not expect her to become a good housekeeper or to take any real interest in her own home. Early training is very important and most of the slovenly housekeeping is the parent's fault.

CAREERS AND AMBITION

It is worth taking the trouble to record in writing impressions of children's reactions to games and hobbies as they are growing up. Such a personal record may well be of great value later on, when the question of careers must be considered.

There are still too many square pegs in round holes; too many people unhappy, discontented and restless doing work they hate because they were forced into it by economic necessity, and did not know 'what else to do'.

Ambition is right; there can be no endeavour without it, no wish for improvement. But we must not only dream of it – we must act. Our children's material ambition should be to succeed at whatever they undertake, to learn to put their whole force and intellect into what they are doing, and ardently to cultivate themselves in all outside matters in their spare time. This is the only way in which they can make the most of their powers and be happy.

Energy, vitality and high spirits must not be mistaken for misbehaviour. A touch of genius gives much trouble before it finds and pursues its particular bent in life.

AND FINALLY, PARENTS ARE ONLY HUMAN

We as parents are only human. We are often too harassed to keep our temper, too tired to be patient, too unhappy ourselves to judge whether our children are happy or not. We lose our temper, we scold our children unfairly, and we get cross with them for things that are often our own fault.

If we are human enough to make mistakes we should be human enough to admit making them, to say, 'It really was my fault, I'm sorry', or 'I know I'm cross today, but I don't feel very well.'

Although it may be disconcerting, it is a good thing on days when we ourselves are behaving badly, to hear even a five-year-old say with affection and concern, 'You don't feel very well today, do you?' This shows that the child has learned already to make allowances for people's behaviour, and in a small way to adapt her own behaviour to other people's needs. It shows that the centre of interest has begun to shift from herself to other people.

Bringing up children is in fact helping the child to make this transition from loving only herself to loving others, from pleasing only herself to giving others pleasure, and from recognizing only her own needs and their satisfaction to acknowledging those of others. If we can do this without destroying her self-confidence, and without deforming her personality by giving her feelings of resentment, inferiority or fear we will have succeeded as parents.